ESSENTIAL EGGS RECIPES

Mags Pie

Disclaimer

This following non-fictional book is intended to provide information and insights based on the available knowledge and research. This book is designed to present general knowledge and perspectives on the topic. It is not intended to replace professional advice.

Finally, the reader understands that this book is protected by copyright laws and unauthorized reproduction, distribution, or transmission of any part of this book, in any form or by any means, without the prior written permission of the author(s) or publisher, is strictly prohibited. By reading this book, the reader acknowledges and agrees to the terms and conditions stated in this disclaimer.

Introduction

Step into the world of culinary mastery with my Grandma's Egg Recipes. The booklet dates back from 1940's and was published as a weekly booklet for the "Cook's Library" edition. It is dedicated to the versatile and beloved ingredient that is the humble egg. This exquisite collection of recipes celebrates the art of egg cookery, presenting a treasure trove of timeless dishes that span cultures and cuisines.

Everyone knows that of all foods - not excluding meat - the egg is the most nutritious and healthiest food.

Eggs that are used for eating are produced by the hen, duck, turkey, goose, guinea fowl, peacock, seagull, pigeon and ostrich. The hen's egg, however, surpasses all in taste and quality. Some prefer the duck egg, not because of its taste, but because it contains more nitrogenous and fatty substances. Apart from their size, the eggs of the turkey and the gosling have no other characteristic. The quail egg is very small, but with a superb taste. So dear to the eccentric desires of Vitellius and Caligula, the peacock's egg has a sweet, sometimes terribly disgusting taste. Seagull eggs, which are abundantly collected on the shores of the Baltic and North Seas, have their convinced fans, despite the rather strong smell of fish oil.

The Arabs consider an ostrich egg soon buried in the sand to be a pleasant feast. Not so big and more delicate, the green cassowary egg is a great food – it has the taste of a goose egg accompanied by a delicate exotic aroma. The delicious taste of the pheasant egg is vaguely reminiscent of the meat of the bird itself. And on the coast of Madagascar and in Tibet there is a trade in turtle eggs, which are in great demand by the Chinese.

Yet the crown falls on the hen's egg. Firstly, because it is cheaper and secondly, it is always at hand.

Egg Symbolism

The symbol of the egg holds significant meaning in mythology and is found in various cultures throughout history. It is often associated with creation, birth, fertility, and the potential for new life. The concept of the cosmic egg, also known as the world egg or the primordial egg, is a recurring motif that represents the origin of the universe or the beginning of all existence. Let's explore its significance in different mythological traditions.

In ancient Egyptian mythology, the cosmic egg was known as the "Ogdoad." It represented the primeval waters from which the sun god Ra emerged, giving birth to the world. The egg symbolized the potential for creation and the cyclical nature of life and death.

Hindu Mythology: Hindu mythology features the concept of the "Hiranyagarbha," which translates to "golden womb" or "golden egg." The Hiranyagarbha represents the cosmic egg from which the universe hatched. It symbolizes the unmanifested potential and the source of all existence. In some versions, Brahma, the creator deity, is believed to have been born from this egg.

In Chinese mythology, the cosmic egg is known as the "Taiji." It represents the harmonious fusion of yin and yang, the opposing forces of the universe. The Taiji egg symbolizes the interconnectedness of all things and the balance between feminine and masculine energies.

In Greek mythology, the cosmic egg is associated with the Orphic tradition and is known as the "Orphic Egg" or "World Egg." According to the Orphic cosmogony, the primordial being Phanes emerged from this egg, bringing about the creation of the gods and the universe. The Orphic Egg symbolizes the generative power and the potential for creation.

In Norse mythology, the cosmic egg is represented by the "Ginnungagap," which means "yawning gap" or "primordial void." The Ginnungagap was the vast emptiness that existed before the creation of the world. Within this void, the primordial giant Ymir emerged, giving rise to the cosmos. Although not depicted as an egg in this mythology, the concept of the cosmic egg can be seen metaphorically in the Ginnungagap as the source of creation.

Various Native American tribes have their own creation stories featuring the cosmic egg symbol. For example, the Ojibwe tribe has a myth where the Earth is formed from the broken shell of a cosmic egg. In other tribes, the cosmic egg represents the womb of the Earth Mother, symbolizing fertility and the birth of all life.

These examples provide a glimpse into the diverse mythological interpretations of the egg symbol. In general, the egg signifies the potential for creation, birth, and the origin of life. It represents the primordial state of existence, from which the universe and all beings emerge. The egg symbolizes the cyclical nature of life, regeneration, and the interconnectedness of all things.

Some Words on Egg Recipes

Fine words butter no parsnips, but they often make an egg taste better.

Eggs are incredibly versatile and can be used in a wide range of beloved recipes. Here are some of the most loved and popular recipes featuring eggs:

Scrambled eggs are a breakfast staple loved by many. Lightly beaten eggs are cooked in a pan with butter or oil, often seasoned with salt and pepper. They can be enjoyed plain or customized with additions like cheese, herbs, or vegetables.

Eggs Benedict: This indulgent brunch dish features a toasted English muffin topped with Canadian bacon or ham, a poached egg, and hollandaise sauce. It's a rich and flavorful combination that has become a brunch favorite.

Omelettes offer endless possibilities for customization. Eggs are beaten, seasoned, and cooked in a pan, then folded over various fillings like cheese, vegetables, herbs, or meats. They can be enjoyed for breakfast, lunch, or dinner.

Quiche is a savory pie made with a crust and a filling of beaten eggs, cream, and a variety of ingredients such as cheese, vegetables, bacon, or seafood. It can be served hot or cold and is a popular dish for brunches, picnics, and gatherings.

Deviled eggs are a classic appetizer or snack. Hard-boiled eggs are halved, and the yolks are mixed with mayonnaise, mustard, and seasonings. The mixture is then spooned back into the egg whites, creating a delicious and creamy bite-sized treat.

Similar to Eggs Benedict, Eggs Florentine features a toasted English muffin topped with sautéed spinach, a poached egg, and hollandaise sauce. It's a delightful variation that adds a healthy dose of greens to the dish.

Frittatas are versatile and easy-to-make egg dishes. They are essentially baked omelettes that can be loaded with various ingredients like vegetables, cheese, herbs, and meats. Frittatas are great for breakfast, brunch, or as a light dinner option.

Shakshuka is a flavorful and spicy dish originating from the Middle East and

North Africa. It typically consists of eggs poached in a simmering tomato sauce with peppers, onions, and aromatic spices. It is often enjoyed with crusty bread for dipping.

Egg Salad Sandwich are a classic lunchtime favorite. Hard-boiled eggs are mashed and mixed with mayonnaise, mustard, herbs, and seasonings. The creamy egg salad is then spread onto bread and paired with lettuce, tomato, or other desired toppings.

Crème Brûlée: This elegant dessert features a rich custard base made with egg yolks, cream, sugar, and vanilla. It is baked until set and chilled, then topped with a layer of caramelized sugar, creating a satisfying contrast between the creamy custard and the crunchy caramel.

These are just a few examples of the most loved recipes with eggs. Eggs are truly versatile and can be enjoyed in countless other dishes, including cakes, cookies, pancakes, and more. Their ability to add flavor, texture, and richness makes them a beloved ingredient in both sweet and savory culinary creations.

Mayonnaise

Mayonnaise, a creamy and versatile condiment enjoyed around the world, has a rich and fascinating history. Its origins can be traced back to the 18th century and are intertwined with the culinary traditions of France and Spain.

The story of mayonnaise begins in the Mediterranean region, specifically in the Spanish city of Mahon on the island of Menorca. During the 18th century,

Menorca was a strategic naval base, and the local cooks prepared a sauce called "salsa mahonesa" to accompany various dishes. This sauce was made by emulsifying egg yolks with olive oil and flavoring it with vinegar or lemon juice.

It is believed that the Duke of Richelieu, a French military leader, tasted this sauce while serving in Menorca during the Seven Years' War. Captivated by its deliciousness, he brought the recipe back to France. The sauce quickly gained popularity in French aristocratic circles, especially in Paris, and underwent some modifications to suit French tastes. The name "mahonesa" gradually evolved into "mayonnaise" in French.

Mayonnaise gained widespread recognition in France during the 19th century, becoming a staple in haute cuisine and a favorite among renowned chefs. The French chef Marie-Antoine

Carême, considered the founder of classical French cuisine, further refined the recipe by incorporating seasonings like mustard and herbs, elevating mayonnaise to new levels of culinary sophistication.

Over time, mayonnaise spread beyond the borders of France, captivating palates worldwide. Its creamy texture, tangy flavor, and versatility made it a beloved condiment in countless culinary traditions. Variations emerged in different countries, incorporating local ingredients and flavor profiles. For example, in the United States, mayonnaise often includes vinegar or lemon juice, while Japanese mayonnaise commonly incorporates rice vinegar and a touch of MSG.

Today, mayonnaise is not only enjoyed as a standalone condiment but is also a key ingredient in numerous recipes, from sandwiches and salads to dressings and sauces. It has become a staple in households, restaurants, and commercial food production.

The history of mayonnaise showcases how a simple sauce originating in a Mediterranean island found its way to international fame, undergoing adaptations and innovations along the way. Its journey highlights the transformative power of culinary exploration and the enduring appeal of a delectable condiment that adds a creamy touch to countless dishes around the world.

Béchamel Sauce

Béchamel sauce, also known as white sauce, is a classic French sauce made from a roux (a mixture of equal parts butter and flour) and milk. It serves as a versatile base for many dishes and is commonly used in lasagnas, gratins, soufflés, and various other recipes. Here is a detailed overview of sauce béchamel:

Ingredients:

2 tablespoons butter

2 tablespoons all-purpose flour

2 cups milk (whole milk or a combination of milk and cream)

Salt, pepper, and nutmeg (to taste)

Instructions:

Melt the butter: In a saucepan over medium heat, melt the butter until it becomes foamy. Be careful not to let it brown.

Add the flour: Sprinkle the flour over the melted butter and whisk continuously to combine. Cook the mixture, known as a roux, for a minute or two until it turns a pale golden color. This cooking process helps remove the raw taste of the flour.

Incorporate the milk: Gradually pour the milk into the saucepan while whisking constantly to prevent lumps from forming. Adding the milk slowly allows it to incorporate smoothly with the roux.

Cook the sauce: Continue whisking the mixture over medium heat until it thickens and comes to a gentle simmer. The sauce should coat the back of a spoon. This process typically takes around 5-7 minutes. Be sure to whisk constantly to avoid any scorching or sticking.

Season the sauce: Season the béchamel sauce with salt, pepper, and a pinch of nutmeg according to your taste preferences. Nutmeg adds a subtle warmth and enhances the flavor of the sauce. Remember to taste and adjust the seasoning as needed.

Strain (optional): If desired, strain the sauce through a fine-mesh sieve to remove any potential lumps or bits of cooked flour. This step helps achieve a smoother consistency.

Usage and variations: Béchamel sauce can be used immediately in recipes, or it can be cooled and stored in the refrigerator for later use. It serves as a base for other sauces such as Mornay sauce (béchamel with cheese) or as an ingredient in various dishes, providing a creamy and rich flavor.

Additional tips:

To prevent lumps, ensure that the flour is thoroughly whisked into the butter before adding the milk.

Adjust the thickness of the sauce by adding more or less milk. For a thicker sauce, reduce the amount of milk, or increase it for a thinner consistency.

If the sauce becomes too thick, you can thin it out by adding a small amount of milk and whisking until the desired consistency is reached.

To reheat the sauce, gently warm it over low heat, whisking occasionally to prevent scorching.

Sauce béchamel is a versatile and fundamental component of French cuisine. By mastering this basic sauce, you can create a wide range of dishes with a creamy and velvety texture.

Eggs à la coque

Eggs à la coque, also known as soft-boiled eggs, are a classic way of preparing eggs that results in a delicately cooked white and a runny yolk. Here are some details and tips to help you achieve the perfect eggs à la coque:

Start with fresh eggs: Fresh eggs are essential for achieving the best results. The whites of fresh eggs will hold their shape better during cooking, resulting in a neater appearance.

Choose the right size and quantity: Select eggs of a similar size to ensure they cook evenly. A standard serving size for eggs à la coque is usually one to two eggs per person.

Boiling the eggs: Place the eggs in a saucepan and add enough water to cover them completely. Bring the water to a gentle boil over medium heat. Avoid a rapid boil, as it may cause the eggs to bounce around and crack. For consistent cooking, it's best to use room temperature eggs.

Timing: The cooking time depends on personal preference and the size of the eggs. As a general guideline, cook small to medium eggs for 4-5 minutes, and larger eggs for 5-6 minutes. Keep in mind that the eggs will continue to cook slightly after being removed from the water, so adjust the cooking time accordingly.

Timing variations: If you prefer a slightly firmer yolk, add an extra minute of cooking time. Conversely, reduce the cooking time by a minute or so for an even runnier yolk. It may require some experimentation to find your preferred level of doneness.

Gentle handling: Use a slotted spoon or egg cup to carefully remove the eggs from the boiling water. Place them into an egg cup or an egg holder with the pointed side facing up. Tap the top of the egg gently with a spoon or knife to create a small crack for easy peeling.

Serving: Eggs à la coque are typically served with buttered toast soldiers. Cut slices of toasted bread into thin strips, which can be dipped into the runny yolk. Sprinkle a pinch of salt and pepper on the egg before eating, if desired.

Enjoy immediately: Soft-boiled eggs are best enjoyed immediately after cooking to fully experience the creamy yolk and the contrast with the slightly set white. Be cautious of the hot eggs when cracking and peeling them.

Remember, the cooking time can vary depending on factors such as the size of the eggs, altitude, and personal preference. It may take a few attempts to find the perfect timing that suits your taste. Practice and patience will help you master the art of preparing delicious eggs à la coque.

Pickled Eggs

Pickled eggs are a popular culinary creation that involves soaking hard-boiled eggs in a brine solution. Here is some information, history, and tips about pickled eggs:

Preparation: Pickled eggs are typically made by hard-boiling eggs until fully cooked and then submerging them in a flavorful brine solution. The brine usually consists of vinegar, water, salt, sugar, and various spices and seasonings. The eggs are left to marinate in the brine for a period of time, usually several days or weeks, to develop their distinctive tangy flavor.

Flavor Variations: Pickled eggs can be customized with different flavor profiles by varying the ingredients in the brine. Common flavorings include garlic, onions, peppercorns, mustard seeds, dill, and various herbs and spices. The brine solution can be sweet, tangy, spicy, or a combination of flavors, depending on personal preference.

History: Pickled eggs have a history that can be traced back centuries. They were a popular preservation method before refrigeration was widely available. Pickling eggs allowed them to be stored for longer periods, extending their shelf life. Pickled eggs have been enjoyed in various cultures around the world, including Europe, the United States, and the United Kingdom.

Culinary Uses: Pickled eggs can be enjoyed as a snack on their own, served as an appetizer, or used as a garnish in salads, sandwiches, or charcuterie boards. They add a tangy and flavorful element to dishes and can be sliced, quartered, or halved for serving. Some people even enjoy them with hot sauce or as a side dish with hearty meals.

Tips: When making pickled eggs, it's important to ensure that the eggs are fully hard-boiled before pickling to prevent any runny yolks. Additionally, it's recommended to use sterile glass jars for pickling to maintain the quality and freshness of the eggs. Properly sealed and refrigerated pickled eggs can be stored for several weeks, and the flavors tend to intensify the longer they marinate.

Variations: Different regions and cultures have their own variations of pickled eggs. For example, British-style pickled eggs are often flavored with malt vinegar and have a bright yellow color due to the addition of turmeric. In the United States, pickled eggs are sometimes prepared with beet juice, giving them a vibrant pink color.

Pickled eggs are a versatile and tangy delicacy that adds a unique twist to traditional egg dishes. Whether you enjoy them as a standalone snack or incorporate them into various recipes, pickled eggs offer a flavorful and satisfying culinary experience.

Classic Egg Salad

Ingredients:

Hard-boiled eggs, peeled and chopped

Mayonnaise

Dijon mustard

Finely chopped celery

Finely chopped red onion

Fresh dill or parsley, chopped (optional)

Salt and pepper to taste

Instructions:

In a bowl, combine the chopped hard-boiled eggs, mayonnaise, Dijon mustard, celery, red onion, and fresh herbs if using.

Mix everything together until well combined.

Season with salt and pepper to taste.

Serve the classic egg salad on bread, in a wrap, or as a topping for salads.

Deviled Egg Salad

Ingredients:

Hard-boiled eggs, peeled and chopped

Mayonnaise

Dijon mustard

Sweet pickle relish

Finely chopped celery

Finely chopped red onion

Paprika for garnish

Salt and pepper to taste

Instructions:

In a bowl, combine the chopped hard-boiled eggs, mayonnaise, Dijon mustard, sweet pickle relish, celery, and red onion.

Mix everything together until well combined.

Season with salt and pepper to taste.

Sprinkle paprika on top for garnish.

Serve the deviled egg salad on bread, crackers, or lettuce cups.

Mediterranean Egg Salad

Ingredients:

Hard-boiled eggs, peeled and chopped

Greek yogurt

Lemon juice

Chopped cucumber

Chopped tomato

Chopped Kalamata olives

Crumbled feta cheese

Chopped fresh herbs (such as parsley, dill, or mint)

Salt and pepper to taste

Instructions:

In a bowl, combine the chopped hard-boiled eggs, Greek yogurt, lemon juice, cucumber, tomato, Kalamata olives, feta cheese, and fresh herbs.

Mix everything together until well combined.

Season with salt and pepper to taste.

Serve the Mediterranean egg salad on pita bread, in a wrap, or as a side dish to grilled meats.

Egg Balls for Soup

Walking on eggs.

The expression descrtibes a situation where one needs to be extremely cautious and delicate, as if walking on fragile eggshells.

Ingredients:

4 eggs

1 tablespoon cornstarch

1/4 teaspoon salt

1/4 teaspoon black pepper

Optional: chopped fresh herbs or grated cheese for flavor variation

Instructions:

In a mixing bowl, crack the eggs and whisk them until well beaten.

Add the cornstarch, salt, and black pepper to the beaten eggs and whisk again until fully combined. The cornstarch helps bind the mixture together and gives the egg balls a slightly firmer texture.

Optional: If you'd like to add additional flavor to the egg balls, you can mix in some chopped fresh herbs like parsley, chives, or cilantro, or even grated cheese such as Parmesan or cheddar.

Heat a pot of water or broth until it reaches a gentle simmer.

Using a spoon or a small ice cream scoop, drop small portions of the egg mixture into the simmering liquid, forming small egg balls. You can make them about 1 inch in diameter.

Let the egg balls cook in the simmering liquid for about 3-5 minutes, or until they are cooked through. They should be firm and set when gently touched.

Use a slotted spoon to remove the cooked egg balls from the pot and transfer them to a bowl or directly into your soup.

Repeat the process until all the egg mixture is used.

Serve the egg balls in your favorite soup or broth. They add a delightful texture and taste to the soup.

You can adjust the seasoning and flavorings according to your preference. These egg balls are versatile and can be added to various soups such as chicken soup, vegetable soup, or even noodle soup. Enjoy!

Scrambled Eggs

Like trying to unscramble an egg.

This expression describes a situation that is virtually impossible or extremely difficult to rectify or undo.

Scrambled eggs have been a popular dish for centuries, but the exact origin is unclear. It is believed that the Romans enjoyed a similar dish called "frictata," which consisted of beaten eggs cooked in a pan. Over time, different cultures and cuisines developed their own versions of scrambled eggs.

Styles of Scrambled Eggs:

Classic Scrambled Eggs: This style involves beating eggs with a fork or whisk, adding a bit of salt and pepper, and cooking them in a pan with butter or oil. The eggs are gently stirred or "scrambled" as they cook until they reach a creamy and slightly runny texture.

French Scrambled Eggs: Also known as "oeufs brouillés," this style involves whisking the eggs with cream or crème fraîche before cooking them slowly over low heat. The result is soft and custardy scrambled eggs with a delicate texture.

American Scrambled Eggs: This style often includes milk or cream in the egg mixture. The eggs are beaten until well combined, cooked over medium heat, and stirred continuously to form small curds. American-style scrambled eggs tend to be slightly firmer and well-cooked.

Tips for Making Scrambled Eggs:

Choose Fresh Eggs: Fresh eggs yield the best results when making scrambled eggs. They have a firmer texture and provide better structure to the dish.

Beat the Eggs Well: Use a whisk or fork to beat the eggs until the yolks and whites are fully incorporated. This step helps create a uniform texture and ensures the eggs cook evenly.

Season Properly: Add salt and pepper to the beaten eggs before cooking. Seasoning the eggs directly enhances their flavor. You can also experiment with other seasonings like herbs, spices, or grated cheese.

Use Low Heat: To achieve creamy scrambled eggs, cook them over low heat. This slower cooking method allows for gentle and even cooking, preventing the eggs from becoming tough or overcooked.

Stir Gently: Use a spatula or wooden spoon to stir the eggs gently as they cook. Continuously moving the eggs around the pan helps create small curds and a fluffy texture.

Remove from Heat Early: It's best to remove the eggs from the heat while they are still slightly runny. They will continue cooking from the residual heat, and this ensures they remain moist and creamy.

Experiment with Ingredients: Don't be afraid to add extra ingredients to your scrambled eggs, such as sautéed vegetables, cheese, herbs, or cooked meats. These additions can enhance the flavor and create a more satisfying meal.

Remember, cooking scrambled eggs is a personal preference, and you can adjust the techniques and ingredients to suit your taste. With practice and experimentation, you'll be able to create perfect scrambled eggs tailored to your liking.

Omelette

The history of the omelette, a delicious and versatile dish made from beaten eggs cooked in a frying pan, is intertwined with the culinary traditions of various cultures throughout history. While it is challenging to pinpoint an exact origin, omelettes have been enjoyed in different forms across different regions for centuries.

Eggs have been consumed by humans since prehistoric times, and the concept of cooking eggs in various ways likely developed early on. The practice of making omelettes can be traced back to ancient Persia (modern-day Iran), where cooks prepared a dish called "kuku," consisting of beaten eggs mixed with various ingredients like vegetables, herbs, and spices before being cooked.

From Persia, the concept of the omelette spread to other parts of the world through trade and cultural exchanges. In ancient Greece, omelettes, known as "orektika," were made with eggs, herbs, and cheese. The Greeks also introduced the idea of folding the omelette over the filling, creating the distinctive half-moon shape.

During the Roman Empire, omelettes gained popularity, and ancient Roman cookbooks feature recipes for "ovemele" or "ovemeleus." These recipes often called for mixing eggs with milk or broth and adding various fillings such as meat, fish, and vegetables. The Romans valued eggs as a versatile ingredient, and their culinary influence helped spread the love for omelettes throughout their vast empire.

As the centuries passed, the popularity of omelettes continued to grow across Europe. In medieval France, omelettes became a part of the culinary repertoire, and French chefs developed a reputation for their skill in preparing exquisite omelettes. Omelettes were often enjoyed by the French aristocracy, and the renowned French chef François Pierre La Varenne featured several omelette recipes in his influential cookbook "Le Cuisinier François" published in 1651.

Throughout the centuries, omelettes have evolved and diversified. Today, they are enjoyed in numerous variations and with an endless array of fillings and flavors. From the classic French omelette made with just eggs, butter, and salt, to Spanish tortillas filled with potatoes and onions, and the fluffy American-style omelettes loaded with cheese, vegetables, and meats, the possibilities are endless.

The history of the omelette showcases how a simple dish made from eggs and basic ingredients has evolved and adapted across cultures and time. It is a testament to the enduring appeal of this versatile culinary creation, loved by people around the world for its simplicity, taste, and endless potential for creativity in the kitchen.

Custard

Custard, a creamy and luscious dessert enjoyed in various forms across the world, has a long and storied history that can be traced back to ancient civilizations.

The origin of custard can be attributed to the ancient Romans, who were known for their culinary prowess. They developed a basic recipe using milk, eggs, and honey, which served as a foundation for custard as we know it today. The Romans valued eggs for their binding properties and used them extensively in their cuisine.

During the Middle Ages, custard gained popularity across Europe. Cooks began incorporating more spices, such as saffron and cinnamon, to enhance the flavor of the custard. It became a favorite among the nobility and was often served as a standalone dessert or used as a filling for tarts and pies.

In the 17th and 18th centuries, custard evolved further as culinary techniques and ingredients advanced. The addition of cream instead of or alongside milk created a richer and more indulgent custard. Cookbook authors of the time, such as François Massialot and Hannah Glasse, included recipes for custard and highlighted its versatility as a dessert.

One of the most famous custard-based desserts is crème anglaise, a classic French custard sauce. It is made by slowly heating milk, sugar, and vanilla and then tempering the mixture with beaten eggs. The resulting sauce is often served alongside or poured over cakes, pastries, or fruits.

In the 19th and 20th centuries, custard continued to be an integral part of culinary traditions around the world. It was adapted and enjoyed in various forms, such as baked custard, custard tarts, and crème brûlée, where a caramelized sugar crust tops the creamy custard base.

Today, custard remains a beloved dessert with countless variations. Different countries and cultures have put their own spin on custard recipes, incorporating local flavors and ingredients. For example, in Asia, custard is often infused with pandan leaves or coconut milk, creating unique flavor profiles.

The history of custard showcases the enduring appeal of this delightful dessert. From its humble origins in ancient Rome to its prominence in the modern culinary landscape, custard has evolved and adapted to suit the tastes and preferences of different eras and cultures. Whether enjoyed warm or chilled, plain or flavored, custard continues to be a cherished treat that brings comfort and satisfaction to dessert lovers worldwide.

Meringue

Meringue, a light and airy confection made from whipped egg whites and sugar, has a fascinating history that dates back several centuries. Its origins can be traced to Europe, particularly Switzerland and France.

The exact origin of meringue is uncertain, but it is believed to have been invented in the late 17th century. The first documented mention of meringue can be found in François Massialot's cookbook "Nouvelle instruction pour les confitures, les liquers et les fruits" published in 1692. However, it's worth noting that similar recipes using whipped egg whites and sugar were known in Italian and Swiss cuisine before that time.

The name "meringue" is said to have originated from the Swiss village of Meiringen, where a local pastry chef named Gasparini created a dessert resembling meringue during a visit by the Polish royal family in the 18th century. The dessert became known as "meringue" as a tribute to the village.

Meringue gained popularity in France during the 18th century, particularly under the reign of King Louis XVI and his queen, Marie Antoinette. Meringue desserts were a favorite at the French court, and they were often served as delicate, sweet confections in various forms.

In the 19th century, meringue experienced further development and refinement. Pastry chefs began experimenting with different shapes and sizes, creating individual meringue shells, pavlovas, and layered cakes. The addition of cornstarch or vinegar to the meringue mixture helped stabilize it and create a crisp outer shell while maintaining a soft and marshmallow-like interior.

One iconic meringue dessert that emerged during this period is the Pavlova, named after the Russian ballerina Anna Pavlova. The pavlova is a meringue-based dessert with a crispy exterior and a soft, marshmallow-like interior, typically topped with whipped cream and fresh fruits. Its creation is often attributed to either Australian or New Zealand culinary traditions, with disputes over the exact origins of the dessert.

Today, meringue desserts come in various forms and flavors. Meringue shells are often used as the base for desserts like Eton Mess, Lemon Meringue Pie, and Baked Alaska. Meringue is also piped and baked into individual cookies known as "meringue kisses" or "meringue drops."

The enduring appeal of meringue desserts lies in their delicate texture, lightness, and versatility. They have become an integral part of pastry and dessert traditions worldwide, delighting taste buds with their airy sweetness and visually appealing presentations.

The history of meringue desserts showcases the artistry and creativity of pastry chefs throughout the centuries. From its humble beginnings as a Swiss confection to its widespread popularity as an essential element of pastry arts, meringue has become a cherished treat enjoyed by dessert enthusiasts around the globe.

Eggs around the Globe

African eggs

Shakshuka is a popular North African dish made with eggs poached in a spiced tomato sauce. It typically includes ingredients such as tomatoes, bell peppers, onions, garlic, and spices like cumin, paprika, and cayenne pepper. The eggs are cracked into the simmering sauce and cooked until the whites are set but the yolks are still runny. Shakshuka is often enjoyed with crusty bread.

Doro Wat is a traditional Ethiopian and Eritrean dish that features chicken simmered in a rich, spicy sauce. Eggs are a key component of this flavorful stew. Hard-boiled eggs are added to the sauce, allowing them to absorb the aromatic flavors of the spices and onions. Doro Wat is often served with injera, a spongy Ethiopian flatbread.

Egg Jollof Rice is a popular West African dish, and eggs can be incorporated into it for added protein. Hard-boiled eggs are often added to the flavorful rice dish, which typically includes ingredients such as tomatoes, onions, bell peppers, spices, and stock. The eggs are usually halved and placed on top of the cooked rice.

Akara, also known as Bean Fritters, is a common street food in many African countries. It is made by blending black-eyed peas or beans with spices, onions, and sometimes peppers. The batter is deep-fried into golden fritters. While eggs are not always added to the batter, some variations incorporate beaten eggs for added richness and texture.

Egg Stew is a versatile dish enjoyed in different parts of Africa. It typically consists of a tomato-based sauce with onions, garlic, and various spices. Eggs are cracked into the simmering stew and cooked until the desired doneness. The stew can be customized with additional vegetables, such as bell peppers, spinach, or okra.

Arab Eggs

Arabic cuisine is known for its vibrant flavours, aromatic spices and diverse culinary traditions. Eggs are often used to enhance texture and taste of the dishes.

Ful Medames: Ful Medames is a traditional Egyptian dish made with cooked fava beans, olive oil, and various seasonings. It is often topped with a poached or fried egg and served as a hearty breakfast or brunch. The creamy beans and flavorful egg combination is delightful.

Fatteh: Fatteh is a layered dish consisting of toasted bread, yogurt, and a variety of toppings, including eggs. The bread is typically soaked in a tangy yogurt sauce and topped with cooked chickpeas, fried eggplant, roasted nuts, and herbs. It is a flavorful and satisfying dish.

Avalon Eggs

Both Scottish and English cuisines feature several traditional egg dishes. Here are a few examples of typical Scottish and English egg dishes:

Scottish Egg: The Scottish Egg is a popular snack or appetizer that consists of a hard-boiled egg wrapped in sausage meat, coated in breadcrumbs, and then deep-fried until golden and crispy. It is a hearty and satisfying dish commonly enjoyed in Scottish cuisine.

Scotch Eggs: Similar to the Scottish Egg, Scotch Eggs are a traditional English dish. They are made by encasing a hard-boiled egg in sausage meat, rolling it in breadcrumbs, and then baking or frying until cooked through. Scotch Eggs are often served as a picnic or pub food.

Egg and Soldiers: A simple yet beloved breakfast dish in both Scotland and England is Egg and Soldiers. It involves soft-boiled eggs served with strips of toasted bread (resembling soldiers) for dipping into the creamy yolk. It is a nostalgic and comforting morning meal.

Egg Mayonnaise Sandwich: Egg Mayonnaise Sandwich is a classic English sandwich filling made with hard-boiled eggs mashed with mayonnaise, seasoned with salt and pepper, and often mixed with chopped herbs or mustard. The mixture is then spread on slices of bread to create a delicious and satisfying sandwich.

Eggs Benedict: While Eggs Benedict is not exclusive to Scottish or English cuisine, it has become a popular brunch dish in both regions. It typically consists of a poached egg served on top of a toasted English muffin, layered with ham or bacon, and topped with hollandaise sauce. It is a rich and indulgent dish that has become a brunch staple.

These are just a few examples of typical Scottish and English egg dishes. Each cuisine offers a variety of ways to enjoy eggs, whether it's in breakfast dishes, snacks, or more elaborate recipes. Eggs are a versatile ingredient and play a significant role in the culinary traditions of both Scotland and England.

Chinese Eggs

Egg Fried Rice (蛋炒饭) is a popular staple in Chinese cuisine. Cooked rice is stir-fried with beaten eggs, diced vegetables, and sometimes meat or shrimp. Soy sauce and other seasonings are added for flavor. It is a versatile dish that can be customized with different ingredients and variations.

Tea Eggs (茶叶蛋) are a common snack or appetizer in Chinese cuisine. Hard-boiled eggs are cracked lightly and simmered in a mixture of tea, soy sauce, and spices such as star anise, cinnamon, and cloves. The resulting marbled pattern on the eggs and the infused flavors make them a visually appealing and flavorful treat.

Steamed Egg Custard (蒸蛋羹), also known as "steamed egg" or "egg tofu," is a delicate and silky dish. Beaten eggs are combined with water or stock, seasoned with salt or soy sauce, and steamed until set. It can be garnished with ingredients like minced meat, mushrooms, or scallions for added flavor and texture.

Thousand-Year-Old Eggs (皮蛋), also called century eggs or preserved eggs, are a unique Chinese delicacy. They are made by preserving eggs in a mixture of clay, ash, salt, quicklime, and rice hulls for several weeks or months. The process results in an egg with a jelly-like texture, a darkened appearance, and a distinctive savory flavor.

Scrambled Eggs with Tomatoes (番茄炒蛋) is a simple and popular dish in Chinese households. Eggs are lightly beaten and scrambled in a hot wok or skillet. Chopped tomatoes are then added and cooked briefly until slightly softened. It is a quick and flavorful dish often enjoyed with steamed rice.

Spring Onion Pancake (葱油饼), or scallion pancake, is a savory Chinese pancake that often includes eggs in the dough. The dough is typically made with flour, water, and sliced spring onions. It is rolled out, folded, and pan-fried until crispy and golden. The addition of eggs adds richness and a tender texture to the pancake.

Japanese Eggs

Tamagoyaki: Tamagoyaki is a rolled Japanese omelette that is a staple in Japanese bento boxes and breakfasts. It is made by whisking together eggs, soy sauce, and sometimes sugar, then rolling thin layers of the mixture in a rectangular pan. Tamagoyaki is typically served sliced into bite-sized pieces.

Chawanmushi is a savory egg custard dish steamed with a flavorful broth. It typically includes ingredients like shrimp, chicken, mushrooms, and vegetables. The custard is delicate and silky, and it is served in small bowls as an appetizer or part of a traditional Japanese meal.

Omurice is a fusion dish that combines Western omelette and Japanese fried rice. It consists of a fluffy omelette wrapped around fried rice that is typically seasoned with ketchup. Omurice is often topped with additional ketchup or a demi-glace sauce and can include ingredients like chicken, vegetables, and mushrooms.

Okonomiyaki is a savory pancake often referred to as "Japanese pizza" or "Japanese pancake." It is made with a batter of eggs, flour, and shredded cabbage, and it can be customized with various fillings such as pork, seafood, vegetables, and cheese. Okonomiyaki is typically topped with a tangy sauce, mayonnaise, bonito flakes, and dried seaweed.

Oyakodon translates to "parent and child bowl" as it features both chicken (the parent) and eggs (the child). It is a comforting rice bowl dish made by simmering chicken, onions, and beaten eggs in a flavorful broth until the eggs are softly set. Oyakodon is served over a bed of steamed rice.

Tamago Kake Gohan is a simple yet popular Japanese breakfast dish. It consists of a bowl of hot steamed rice topped with a raw egg and seasoned with soy sauce or other condiments. The heat from the rice partially cooks the egg, creating a creamy and comforting meal.

These are just a few examples of the many delightful Japanese recipes that showcase the versatility and deliciousness of eggs. Japanese cuisine often highlights the natural flavors of ingredients while maintaining a delicate balance, and eggs play an essential role in achieving that balance in many dishes.

Latin Eggs

Frittata is an Italian omelette made with beaten eggs mixed with various ingredients such as vegetables, cheese, herbs, or cooked meats. It is cooked in a skillet on the stovetop and often finished under the broiler to set the top. Frittatas are versatile and can be served hot or cold, making them great for any meal.

Carbonara is a famous pasta dish from Rome that features eggs as a key ingredient. The sauce is made by whisking together eggs, grated cheese (typically Pecorino Romano), black pepper, and sometimes cream. The cooked pasta is then tossed in the sauce, creating a creamy and rich dish.

Torta Pasqualina is an Italian Easter pie that traditionally includes layers of phyllo pastry or puff pastry filled with spinach, ricotta cheese, and whole eggs. The eggs cook as the pie bakes, resulting in beautiful slices with a runny yolk center.

Tortilla Española or Spanish omelette, is a classic Spanish dish made with eggs, potatoes, and onions. The potatoes and onions are sautéed until tender and mixed with beaten eggs. The mixture is then cooked in a skillet until set and golden brown on both sides. Tortilla Española is often served in wedges as a tapa or as a filling for sandwiches.

Huevos Rotos, meaning "broken eggs," is a simple and delicious Spanish dish. It consists of fried eggs served on top of crispy fried potatoes (often known as "patatas bravas") and sometimes accompanied by crispy cured ham (jamón serrano or jamón ibérico). The eggs are broken with a fork, allowing the yolk to mix with the potatoes.

Pisto is a Spanish vegetable medley similar to ratatouille. It typically includes tomatoes, onions, bell peppers, and zucchini, sautéed in olive oil until tender. Eggs are cracked into the mixture and cooked until the whites are set and the yolks are still slightly runny. Pisto with eggs is a flavorful and hearty dish often served for breakfast or brunch.

Pastéis de Nata, also known as Portuguese custard tarts, are one of the most beloved Portuguese desserts. These small, flaky pastries consist of a crisp puff pastry shell filled with a creamy egg custard filling flavored with vanilla and cinnamon. They are typically served warm with a sprinkle of powdered sugar and cinnamon on top.

Bacalhau à Brás is a popular Portuguese dish made with salted codfish, eggs, onions, and thinly sliced potatoes. The codfish is first boiled to remove excess salt, then shredded and cooked with onions and garlic. Thinly sliced potatoes are fried until golden and mixed with the codfish. Beaten eggs are added to bind the ingredients together, creating a delicious and hearty dish.

Pudim Flan is a Portuguese version of caramel flan or crème caramel. It is a creamy custard dessert made with eggs, milk, sugar, and vanilla extract. The caramel sauce is prepared by melting sugar until golden and coating the bottom of a baking dish. The custard mixture is poured over the caramel and baked until set. Once cooled, the dessert is inverted onto a serving plate, revealing the caramel on top.

Ovos Moles, which translates to "soft eggs," is a traditional sweet treat from the Aveiro region of Portugal. It is made by combining egg yolks and sugar syrup, which is cooked until it reaches a soft and creamy consistency. The mixture is then piped into various shapes, such as shells or fruits, and typically covered in a thin wafer. Ovos Moles have a rich and sweet flavor, and they are often enjoyed during festive occasions.

Bolo de Laranja is a traditional Portuguese orange cake made with eggs, flour, sugar, and freshly squeezed orange juice and zest. The batter is mixed until smooth and baked until golden. The result is a moist and citrusy cake that can be served plain or topped with a dusting of powdered sugar.

Mexican Eggs

Mexican cuisine has several popular egg dishes that are enjoyed throughout the country. One well-known Mexican egg dish is Huevos Rancheros. Here's some information about it:

Huevos Rancheros, which translates to "rancher's eggs," is a traditional Mexican breakfast dish that is both flavorful and satisfying. It typically consists of fried eggs served on a tortilla and topped with a spicy tomato-based sauce. Here's a general recipe for making Huevos Rancheros:

Ingredients:

Corn tortillas

Eggs

Tomato sauce or salsa

Onion, finely chopped

Jalapeños or other chili peppers, diced (optional)

Garlic, minced

Cilantro, chopped

Refried beans (optional)

Queso fresco or Mexican cheese (optional)

Avocado slices (optional)

Salt and pepper to taste

Instructions:

Heat a small amount of oil in a skillet over medium heat. Fry the tortillas on both sides until they become slightly crispy. Set them aside on a paper towel to drain excess oil.

In the same skillet, add a little more oil if needed and sauté the chopped onion, garlic, and diced chili peppers until they become fragrant.

Pour in the tomato sauce or salsa and simmer for a few minutes until the flavors meld together. Season with salt and pepper to taste.

In a separate pan, fry the eggs to your desired doneness (commonly sunny-side up or over-easy).

To assemble, place a fried tortilla on a plate and spread a spoonful of refried beans, if using, on top. Place a fried egg on the tortilla and spoon the tomato sauce or salsa over the egg.

Garnish with chopped cilantro, crumbled queso fresco or Mexican cheese, and avocado slices if desired.

Serve the Huevos Rancheros hot and enjoy!

Huevos Rancheros can be accompanied by rice, beans, or additional toppings like sour cream or guacamole. It's a hearty and delicious breakfast dish that showcases the vibrant flavors of Mexican cuisine.

Please note that there can be variations in the recipe and preparation methods for Huevos Rancheros depending on regional preferences and personal tastes.

Persian Eggs

Kuku: Kuku is a traditional Iranian egg-based dish similar to an herb frittata or a baked omelette. It is made by combining beaten eggs with chopped herbs such as parsley, cilantro, and dill. Additional ingredients such as spinach, walnuts, barberries, or potatoes may be included for variation. The mixture is then cooked in a skillet or baked in the oven until set.

Shirin Nargesi: Shirin Nargesi, also known as Persian sweet spinach and egg dish, is a popular breakfast or brunch dish in Iran. It combines sautéed spinach with caramelized onions and lightly beaten eggs. The eggs are added to the spinach and onion mixture, creating a flavorful and nutritious dish that is typically served with bread.

Mirza Ghassemi: Mirza Ghassemi is a classic Persian dish originating from the Gilan province. It is made with grilled or roasted eggplant, tomatoes, garlic, and eggs. The eggplant is first cooked until soft and then mixed with tomatoes and garlic, creating a smoky and aromatic base. Eggs are added and cooked until they are lightly scrambled and mixed with the other ingredients. Mirza Ghassemi is often served with rice or flatbread.

Khagineh: Khagineh, sometimes referred to as Persian omelette, is a simple and versatile dish made with beaten eggs. The eggs are lightly seasoned with salt and pepper and cooked in a frying pan until set. It can be enjoyed plain or with additional ingredients such as onions, herbs, or tomatoes for added flavor.

Eggs in Stews: Eggs are often incorporated into Persian stews to add richness and protein. They can be added whole, poached, or hard-boiled, depending on the specific recipe. For instance, in dishes like Ghormeh Sabzi (herb stew) or Fesenjan (pomegranate walnut stew), eggs are sometimes added toward the end of the cooking process to infuse the flavors of the stew.

In Iranian cuisine, eggs are utilized in various dishes, from breakfast options to main courses and stews. They contribute flavor, texture, and protein to these culinary creations, making them an integral part of the rich and diverse Iranian gastronomy.

Thai Eggs

Thai egg recipe is called "Kai Jeow" or Thai-style omelet. It is a simple and delicious dish that can be enjoyed as a main course or served alongside other Thai dishes. Here's a recipe for Kai Jeow:

Ingredients:

2-3 large eggs

2 tablespoons fish sauce

1 tablespoon soy sauce

1 teaspoon sugar

1/4 cup finely chopped onions

1/4 cup finely chopped tomatoes

1/4 cup chopped green onions (scallions)

Vegetable oil for frying

Fresh cilantro leaves (optional, for garnish)

Thai sweet chili sauce (for serving)

Instructions:

In a mixing bowl, beat the eggs lightly with a fork or whisk.

Add fish sauce, soy sauce, and sugar to the beaten eggs. Mix well until combined.

Stir in the chopped onions, tomatoes, and green onions, and gently mix everything together.

Heat oil in a frying pan or wok over medium heat.

Once the oil is hot, pour the egg mixture into the pan, spreading it evenly to form a round omelet shape.

Allow the omelet to cook for a couple of minutes until the bottom is golden brown and set.

Carefully flip the omelet using a spatula and cook the other side until golden brown and cooked through.

Once cooked, transfer the omelet to a serving plate.

Garnish with fresh cilantro leaves if desired.

Serve hot with Thai sweet chili sauce on the side for dipping.

You can enjoy Kai Jeow with steamed rice and other Thai dishes for a complete meal.

Kai Jeow is a versatile dish, and you can also add other ingredients such as minced meat, shrimp, or vegetables to customize it to your liking. It's a flavorful and satisfying Thai egg recipe that is quick and easy to make.

Turkish Eggs

Turkish cuisine offers a variety of delicious egg recipes that are both flavorful and popular among locals and visitors alike. Here's some information about Turkish egg recipes, as well as the traditional Turkish wedding egg soup:

Menemen is a popular Turkish breakfast dish made with eggs, tomatoes, green peppers, onions, and various spices. It is a flavorful and hearty dish that is typically cooked in a skillet or pan. The vegetables are sautéed until soft, and then the eggs are added and lightly scrambled within the mixture. Menemen is often enjoyed with crusty bread for a satisfying breakfast.

Cilbir is a classic Turkish dish consisting of poached eggs served on a bed of garlicky yogurt sauce and drizzled with melted butter infused with red pepper flakes. It is traditionally enjoyed for breakfast or brunch. The combination of creamy yogurt, runny eggs, and flavorful butter creates a delightful blend of textures and flavors.

Pide with Eggs (Yumurtalı Pide) is a popular Turkish flatbread that can be topped with various ingredients, including eggs. Yumurtalı Pide refers to pide topped with cracked eggs and baked until the eggs are cooked to your preference. The result is a delicious combination of soft bread, savory toppings, and perfectly cooked eggs.

Turkish Wedding Egg Soup (Düğün Çorbası): The Turkish Wedding Egg Soup is a traditional soup often served at weddings and special occasions. It is a comforting and rich soup made with chicken broth, rice, lemon juice, and eggs. The eggs are beaten and slowly added to the hot soup, creating ribbons of cooked egg throughout the broth. It is typically garnished with fresh herbs and served as a starter during celebratory events.

Snow Eggs

Snow eggs, also known as îles flottantes or floating islands, are a delightful sweet dish consisting of poached meringue floating on a bed of creamy custard. They are a classic French dessert that is light, elegant, and visually appealing. Here is some information about snow eggs:

Preparation:

Custard: The base of snow eggs is a velvety custard. It is typically made with milk, sugar, and egg yolks, which are gently heated together until thickened. Vanilla is often added for flavoring.

Meringue: The meringue for snow eggs is made from egg whites and sugar. The egg whites are whipped until stiff peaks form, and sugar is gradually incorporated. The meringue mixture is then poached in simmering water to cook the exterior while maintaining a soft and fluffy interior.

Assembly:

Poaching the Meringue: Using a large spoon or piping bag, dollops or quenelles of meringue are carefully placed into simmering water. The meringue is gently poached until cooked through, which usually takes a few minutes per side. The poached meringue is then transferred to a paper towel-lined plate to drain excess water.

Custard Bed: The chilled custard is poured into serving bowls or glasses to create a base for the floating islands.

Placing the Meringue: The poached meringue is delicately placed on top of the custard, resembling floating clouds or islands. The meringue should be light and fluffy, adding an airy and ethereal touch to the dessert.

Caramel or Sauce (Optional): Snow eggs can be served plain, but they are often accompanied by a drizzle of caramel sauce, chocolate sauce, or fruit compote for added sweetness and flavor.

Variations and Serving:

Flavored Custard: The custard can be infused with various flavors such as citrus zest, cinnamon, or almond extract to add depth and complexity to the dessert.

Crème Anglaise: Instead of a plain custard, some versions of snow eggs use crème anglaise, a rich and creamy sauce made with egg yolks, sugar, and vanilla. The meringue floats on top of the smooth sauce.

Snow eggs are a delightful and elegant dessert, perfect for special occasions or as a light and refreshing treat. The combination of the fluffy poached meringue and creamy custard creates a lovely contrast in textures and flavors. Its name, "snow eggs," comes from the resemblance of the meringue islands to soft, pillowy snowflakes.

Caramel flan, also known as crème caramel, is a popular dessert enjoyed in many countries around the world. It is a smooth and creamy custard dessert topped with a layer of golden caramel sauce. Here is some information about caramel flan:

Preparation:

Caramel Sauce: The first step in making caramel flan is preparing the caramel sauce. Granulated sugar is heated in a saucepan until it melts and turns amber in color. The caramel is then poured into the bottom of a baking dish or individual ramekins, allowing it to coat the bottom evenly.

Custard: The custard for caramel flan is made with a mixture of eggs, milk, and sugar. Vanilla extract or other flavorings like citrus zest or liqueur can be added for extra flavor. The ingredients are combined and gently whisked until well blended but not overly frothy.

Baking: The custard mixture is poured over the caramel in the baking dish or ramekins. The dish is then placed in a water bath, which helps to ensure gentle and even cooking. The water bath provides insulation and prevents the custard from curdling or overcooking.

Cooking: The flan is baked in the oven at a moderate temperature until set. The cooking time can vary depending on the size of the dish or ramekins. It usually takes about 45 minutes to an hour. The custard should have a slight jiggle in the center when gently shaken.

Chilling and Unmolding: Once cooked, the caramel flan is removed from the oven and left to cool to room temperature. It is then refrigerated for several hours or overnight to fully set. Just before serving, the flan is unmolded by carefully inverting the dish onto a serving plate, allowing the caramel sauce to flow over the custard.

Variations:

Flavorings: While vanilla is the most common flavoring for caramel flan, you can experiment with different extracts or infusions such as coffee, chocolate, almond, or coconut to add a unique twist to the dessert.

Individual Portions: Caramel flan can be made in individual ramekins for individual servings, which is a charming presentation option for dinner parties or gatherings.

Garnishes: Caramel flan is often served plain, but it can be accompanied by whipped cream, fresh berries, or a dusting of powdered sugar for added visual appeal and flavor.

Caramel flan is a luscious and elegant dessert that combines the creamy richness of the custard with the bittersweet caramel sauce. Its smooth texture and sweet flavors make it a beloved treat enjoyed by many cultures around the world.

Crepe Suzette

Egg on your nest.

This saying conveys the idea of encouraging or provoking someone to take action or face a challenge.

Crepe Suzette is a classic French dessert made with thin, delicate crepes that are served with a sweet and tangy orange sauce. Here are more details about Crepe Suzette, including its history and a recipe:

History: Crepe Suzette is believed to have been created in the late 19th century by French chef Auguste Escoffier. The story goes that Escoffier was preparing a dessert for the Prince of Wales, who later became King Edward VII of England. While making traditional crepes, Escoffier accidentally flambéed them with Grand Marnier liqueur, resulting in a flavorful and caramelized sauce. The prince loved the creation and asked for it to be named after a young woman who was dining with him, Suzette. Since then, Crepe Suzette has become a classic French dessert enjoyed worldwide.

Recipe: Crepe Suzette

Ingredients: For the crepes:

1 cup all-purpose flour

2 tablespoons sugar

1/4 teaspoon salt

3 large eggs

1 1/4 cups milk

2 tablespoons melted butter

Butter or oil for greasing the pan

For the sauce:

Zest of 2 oranges

Juice of 4 oranges (about 1 cup)

1/4 cup sugar

1/4 cup Grand Marnier or other orange liqueur

4 tablespoons unsalted butter, cut into pieces

Optional garnish:

Orange segments

Whipped cream

Fresh mint leaves

Instructions:

In a mixing bowl, whisk together the flour, sugar, and salt. Make a well in the center.

In another bowl, whisk together the eggs, milk, and melted butter. Pour the mixture into the well of the dry ingredients.

Gradually whisk the wet and dry ingredients together until you have a smooth batter. Let the batter rest for about 15 minutes to allow the gluten to relax.

Heat a non-stick skillet or crepe pan over medium heat. Lightly grease the surface with butter or oil.

Pour a small ladleful of batter into the hot pan, swirling it around to evenly coat the bottom. Cook for about 1-2 minutes, until the edges are lightly golden. Flip the crepe and cook for another 1 minute. Repeat with the remaining batter.

Stack the cooked crepes on a plate and keep them warm.

For the sauce, combine the orange zest, orange juice, sugar, and Grand Marnier in a saucepan. Heat over medium heat until the sugar has dissolved and the mixture comes to a simmer.

Reduce the heat to low and add the butter, one piece at a time, whisking constantly until the sauce thickens slightly and becomes glossy.

To serve, fold the crepes into quarters and arrange them on serving plates. Drizzle the warm sauce over the crepes.

If desired, garnish with orange segments, a dollop of whipped cream, and fresh mint leaves.

Serve immediately and enjoy the luscious combination of flavors.

Crepe Suzette is not only delicious but also offers a touch of elegance to any special occasion. The combination of delicate crepes, citrusy orange sauce, and a hint of liqueur creates a delightful and indulgent dessert experience.

Pancakes

Pancakes are a popular breakfast food enjoyed in many cultures around the world. They are made from a simple batter of flour, eggs, milk, and a leavening agent, cooked on a hot surface to create a flat, round, and fluffy cake-like texture. Here's some detailed information, history, and a classic recipe for pancakes:

History: The origin of pancakes can be traced back to ancient times. Archaeological evidence suggests that early civilizations in both the East and West were making some form of pancake-like dish. For example, ancient Greeks and Romans made a type of pancake called "taganites" using wheat flour, olive oil, honey, and curdled milk.

In the Middle Ages, pancakes became a popular dish throughout Europe, often associated with religious festivals such as Shrove Tuesday or Pancake Day. Today, pancakes are enjoyed in various forms and flavors worldwide.

Recipe: Classic Pancakes

Ingredients:

1 cup all-purpose flour

2 tablespoons sugar

2 teaspoons baking powder

1/2 teaspoon salt

1 cup milk

1 large egg

2 tablespoons melted butter or vegetable oil

Optional: vanilla extract, cinnamon, or other flavorings

Instructions:

In a mixing bowl, whisk together the flour, sugar, baking powder, and salt.

In a separate bowl, whisk together the milk, egg, and melted butter or oil. You can also add vanilla extract or other flavorings if desired.

Pour the wet ingredients into the dry ingredients and stir until just combined. It's okay if there are a few lumps in the batter; overmixing can result in tough pancakes.

Heat a non-stick skillet or griddle over medium heat. Lightly grease the surface with butter or oil.

Pour a scoop (about 1/4 cup) of the batter onto the hot surface for each pancake. Cook until bubbles form on the surface and the edges start to look set, about 2-3 minutes.

Flip the pancake and cook for an additional 1-2 minutes, or until golden brown and cooked through.

Transfer the cooked pancakes to a plate and keep warm. Repeat the process with the remaining batter.

Serve the pancakes warm with your choice of toppings such as maple syrup, fresh fruits, whipped cream, or chocolate chips.

Variations and Tips:

You can customize your pancakes by adding ingredients such as blueberries, sliced bananas, chopped nuts, or chocolate chips to the batter.

For healthier options, you can use whole wheat flour or incorporate alternative flours like buckwheat or almond flour.

Experiment with different toppings like honey, fruit preserves, yogurt, or savory options like bacon and cheese.

To keep pancakes warm while cooking the entire batch, place them on a baking sheet in a low-temperature oven (around 200°F or 95°C).

Avoid pressing down on the pancakes with a spatula while cooking, as this can flatten them and make them denser.

Pancakes are a versatile and beloved breakfast staple, offering endless possibilities for creativity and personalization. Whether enjoyed plain, stacked high with toppings, or served alongside bacon and eggs, pancakes are a delightful treat for any time of day.

Egg Drinks and Cocktails

Egg drinks and cocktails, also known as "flips" or "egg flips," have a long history and are still enjoyed today. These beverages typically include eggs as a key ingredient, adding richness and a creamy texture. Here's some information, history, and a classic recipe for an egg-based cocktail:

History: Egg-based drinks have been enjoyed for centuries. The term "flip" originated in England in the late 1600s and referred to a mixture of beer, spirits, sugar, and a hot iron tool called a "loggerhead" that was used to heat and froth the drink. Over time, flips evolved to include eggs, sugar, and spirits, served cold or hot. In the 19th and early 20th centuries, flips became popular in America and were often enjoyed as a morning or holiday beverage. Today, egg drinks and cocktails continue to be appreciated for their unique flavor and texture.

Classic Recipe: Brandy Flip

Ingredients:

2 ounces brandy

1 whole egg

1 tablespoon sugar (or to taste)

Nutmeg, for garnish

Instructions:

In a cocktail shaker, combine the brandy, whole egg, and sugar.

Shake vigorously for about 15 seconds to thoroughly mix and emulsify the ingredients.

Fill the shaker with ice and shake again for about 10 seconds to chill the mixture.

Strain the cocktail into a glass.

Grate fresh nutmeg over the top as a garnish.

Serve and enjoy!

Note: It's important to use fresh, high-quality eggs for egg-based drinks. To ensure safety, you can use pasteurized eggs or consider using a method to pasteurize the eggs at home.

Variations and Tips:

Other spirits such as rum, whiskey, or bourbon can be used instead of brandy to create different flavor profiles.

Sweeteners like simple syrup or maple syrup can be substituted for sugar.

To add extra flavor, you can incorporate ingredients such as vanilla extract, chocolate syrup, or flavored liqueurs.

For a frothy texture, you can use a blender or mix the ingredients with a whisk instead of shaking.

Some recipes call for separating the egg yolk from the white, mixing them separately, and then combining them for a layered effect.

Egg drinks can also be enjoyed warm by heating the mixture gently in a saucepan, but be cautious not to overcook or curdle the eggs.

Egg-based drinks and cocktails provide a unique and indulgent experience. While their popularity has fluctuated over the years, they remain a classic choice for those seeking a rich, creamy, and well-balanced libation.

Egg Coffee

Yes, there is a popular drink that combines egg and coffee called "Egg Coffee." It is a specialty beverage that originated in Vietnam and has gained popularity worldwide. Here's some information and a recipe for Vietnamese Egg Coffee:

History: Egg Coffee, known as "cà phê trứng" in Vietnamese, was invented in the 1940s in Hanoi, Vietnam. Due to a scarcity of milk at the time, Nguyen Van Giang, a local bartender, came up with the idea of using whisked eggs as a substitute. The result was a creamy and rich coffee drink that became a beloved specialty in Vietnamese coffee culture.

Recipe: Vietnamese Egg Coffee

Ingredients:

2 tablespoons Vietnamese coffee (or any strong coffee)

2 tablespoons sweetened condensed milk

1 egg yolk

Hot water

Instructions:

Brew a cup of Vietnamese coffee using a traditional Vietnamese coffee filter or any other method that produces a strong and flavorful coffee concentrate.

In a separate bowl, whisk the egg yolk until smooth and creamy.

Add the sweetened condensed milk to the egg yolk and continue whisking until the mixture is well combined and slightly frothy.

Pour the hot coffee into a cup or glass, filling it about halfway.

Gently spoon the egg and condensed milk mixture on top of the coffee, allowing it to float.

Optionally, you can dust the top with a sprinkle of cocoa powder or cinnamon for added flavor and presentation.

Stir the layers together just before drinking to combine the rich coffee flavor with the creamy egg mixture.

Sip and enjoy the unique blend of flavors and textures.

Egg Coffee is known for its velvety smooth texture and the combination of sweetened condensed milk and the richness of the egg yolk adds a luxurious creaminess to the coffee. It is a delightful treat for coffee lovers who enjoy a touch of sweetness and a unique twist in their beverage.

Note: Vietnamese Egg Coffee is traditionally served hot, but some variations also exist where it is served over ice for a refreshing twist.

Egg Coffee showcases the creativity and ingenuity of Vietnamese coffee culture, offering a distinctive and indulgent way to enjoy your daily cup of joe.

Fabergé Egg

The history of Fabergé eggs is closely tied to the renowned House of Fabergé, a Russian jewelry firm known for its exquisite craftsmanship and intricate designs. The Fabergé eggs are among the most celebrated and iconic creations of this renowned company.

The story of Fabergé eggs begins in the late 19th century when Tsar Alexander III of Russia commissioned Peter Carl Fabergé to create an Easter egg as a gift for his wife, Empress Maria Feodorovna. The result was the first Imperial Fabergé Easter Egg, known as the "Hen Egg," crafted in 1885. This egg had a white enamel shell that opened to reveal a gold yolk containing a golden hen and a tiny diamond replica of the Imperial Crown.

The Hen Egg was so well-received that Alexander III continued the tradition of gifting Fabergé eggs to the empress and his mother, Dowager Empress Maria Feodorovna, every Easter. Each year, a new egg was created with intricate designs, precious metals, gemstones, and hidden surprises.

Fabergé eggs became a symbol of luxury, artistry, and Imperial patronage. The eggs were highly sought after, not only by the Russian Imperial family but also by wealthy collectors around the world. Fabergé's work captivated people with its exquisite beauty and the meticulous craftsmanship involved in creating these small marvels.

In total, 50 Imperial Fabergé Easter Eggs were created from 1885 to 1917. Each egg was unique, and the designs ranged from nature-inspired motifs to historical and religious themes. Fabergé employed various techniques such as enameling, goldsmithing, gem-setting, and miniature painting to bring these treasures to life. Many eggs contained surprises inside, such as miniature portraits, clocks, automata, or delicate figures.

Unfortunately, the Russian Revolution of 1917 led to the downfall of the Romanov dynasty and the House of Fabergé. The imperial eggs were confiscated by the Bolsheviks, and the

Fabergé workshops were closed. Peter Carl Fabergé himself left Russia and settled in Switzerland, where he passed away in 1920.

Over the years, the fate of the Fabergé eggs varied. Some were sold, some were lost, and others were preserved in museums or private collections. The value and significance of these eggs continued to grow, and today, Fabergé eggs are considered priceless works of art.

In recent times, efforts have been made to locate and restore the missing Fabergé eggs, and replicas and modern interpretations of the eggs have been created by the House of Fabergé.

The Fabergé eggs remain a testament to the unparalleled craftsmanship and artistic excellence of the House of Fabergé. They embody the opulence and grandeur of the Russian Imperial court and continue to captivate art enthusiasts and collectors worldwide.